BINGO MATH

Fun-Filled Reproducible Games That Reinforce Essential Math Skills

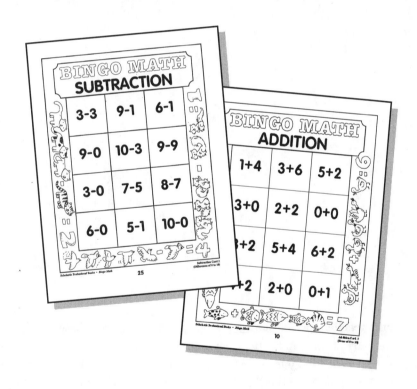

SCHOLASTIC
PROFESSIONAL BOOKS

NEW YORK • TORONTO • LONDON • AUCKLAND • SYDNEY •
MEXICO CITY • NEW DELHI • HONG KONG

For:
Margaret Esposito
Jean Kampfer
Andrea Sullivan
and
Diane Tedeschi

Children are nervous when the new school year starts,
They want teachers with not just great minds, but kind hearts.
So when children find out that these teachers are theirs,
They're heard yelling, "Bingo!" through hallways and stairs!

Cover design by Jaime Lucero
Cover and interior art by Rusty Fletcher
Interior design by Grafica, Inc.
ISBN: 0-590-10962-6

Contents

Introduction 5

How to Play 5

Directions for Individual Game Sets 6

Ways to Win at Bingo 9

GAME SET 1 – Sums of 0 to 10

Bingo Boards 10

Calling Cards 16

GAME SET 2 – Sums of 10 to 20

Bingo Boards 17

Calling Cards 23

GAME SET 3 – Differences of 0 to 10

Bingo Boards 24

Calling Cards 30

GAME SET 4 – Differences of 10 to 20

Bingo Boards 31

Calling Cards 37

GAME SET 5 – Two-Dimensional Shapes

Bingo Boards 38

Calling Cards 44

GAME SET 6 – Three Dimensional Shapes

Bingo Boards 45

Calling Cards 51

GAME SET 7 – Simple Fractions

Bingo Boards 52

Calling Cards 58

GAME SET 8 – Time Showing the Hour and the Half Hour

Bingo Boards 59

Calling Cards 65

GAME SET 9 – Time Showing a Quarter Of and a Quarter After the Hour

Bingo Boards 66

Calling Cards 72

GAME SET 10 – Money/Counting Coins

Bingo Boards 73

Calling Cards 79

GAME SET 11 – Money/Counting Dollar Bills and Coins

Bingo Boards 80

Calling Cards 86

GAME SET 12 – Greater Than/Less Than

Bingo Boards 87

Calling Cards 93

Reproducible Tokens 94

Blank Bingo Board 95

Blank Calling Cards 96

Introduction

There is no doubt about it, Bingo is a fun and exciting game that children love. The reproducible games in *Bingo Math* help make the most of this "kid appeal" by reinforcing essential math skills and concepts in a fun and interactive way. What's more, students will also develop critical-thinking skills as they build strategies for winning.

Each game set includes six different reproducible game boards and a sheet of calling cards. There is a blank bingo board for you and your students to customize (page 95), a page of blank calling cards (page 96), and a page of reproducible tokens (page 94).

In the pages that follow, you'll find general directions for playing the games with one to seven players as well as specific tips and suggestions for enhancing particular games. Here, too, you'll find ideas on how to extend every student's learning experience—whatever his learning style or strength—beyond "Bingo!"

HOW TO PLAY

Whether your students play the games individually, in small groups, or as a whole class, you'll need to photocopy a board for each player and copy and cut apart the calling card page. You may also want to include a copy of possible winning alignments (page 9) and a big supply of buttons, dried beans, or the reproducible tokens found in this book (page 94). Students may enjoy coloring their bingo cards and the reproducible tokens. You can make the game board and pieces more durable by pasting them onto oaktag or cardboard or by laminating them.

Regardless of how you and your students decide to play, you'll want to point out to them that while each reproducible game board (with the exception of those for the time games) contains more than one way to make a particular match, they cannot cover more than one square at a time, nor can they move a token once they have played it. So if a student were playing an addition game and he had two number sentences that yielded the answer 9 (6+3 and 4+5) he would need to decide which sentence to cover to increase his chances of winning. This "secondary" challenge will help kids build all important problem-solving skills as they practice computation.

Solitary Play

If a child wishes to play alone either in a learning center or at his desk, he can set up the game for himself using a single bingo board, the corresponding calling cards, and some tokens. Before he begins playing, the child should decide which token alignment will win the game for him. To play, the player picks a card from the deck and turns it faceup, looking to his bingo board to see if he can make a match. If he does find a match, he covers that space with a token and sets the calling card aside. Play continues in this fashion until the player gets the winning alignment. More advanced players may want to play against themselves using two or more bingo boards.

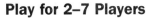

Play for 2–7 Players

The instructions are essentially the same as those for a single player, the only exception being that when there are seven players, one must take on the role of the card caller. If two children play, they can take turns being the card caller. If three to six children play, they may either choose one player to be the card caller or they may each have a bingo board and take turns choosing calling cards in a round-robin fashion. If players go through all the cards without reaching Bingo, they should reshuffle the cards, turn them facedown again, and continue playing until someone has won.

Cooperative Play

Children can also play in teams or pairs. Cooperative play is particularly useful in building students' abilities to communicate well with one another, to share their knowledge, and to learn from their peers.

DIRECTIONS FOR INDIVIDUAL GAME SETS

Game Set 1 (Sums of 0–10) and Game Set 2 (Sums of 10–20)

These game sets include bingo boards with number sentences and calling cards with corresponding sums. In order to place a token on their boards, players must identify a number sentence that yields the calling card sum.

Beyond Bingo

• Invite students to use manipulatives to show the number sentences on each bingo board. Or have them illustrate the number sentences directly on their boards.

• Invite students to create their own addition bingo games by using the blank calling cards (page 96) and bingo boards (page 95).

• Have students create and illustrate story problems using the number sentences on their bingo boards.

Game Set 3 (Differences of 0–10) Game Set 4 (Differences of 10–20)

These game sets include bingo boards with number sentences and calling cards with corresponding differences. In order to place a token on their boards, players must identify a number sentence that yields that difference.

Beyond Bingo

• Invite your students to use manipulatives or their own drawings to illustrate the number sentences on their bingo boards.

• Have children list as many number sentences as they can think of to arrive at a particular difference.

• Challenge students to make up subtraction story problems using the equations on their bingo boards.

Game Set 5 (Two-Dimensional Shapes)

Children match simple line drawings to real-life two-dimensional shapes on their bingo boards.

Beyond Bingo

• Photocopy an extra set of calling cards and invite students to use them to make calling card cutouts. Paste the calling card sheet onto a piece of cardboard or a manila folder for added durability. Then cut out the calling card shapes to allow for more tactile learning. Before students mark a shape on their bingo boards, have

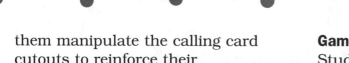

them manipulate the calling card cutouts to reinforce their understanding of these shapes.

• Invite students to customize their bingo boards by filling the spaces with cutouts photos of objects from old magazines and junk mail that correspond to the shapes on their calling cards.

• Have students give verbal clues about the shapes that appear on the calling cards. For example, if a card shows a circle, a student might say, "I have no beginning and no end."

Game Set 6
(Three-Dimensional Shapes)
Children match simple line drawings to real-life three-dimensional shapes on their bingo boards.

Beyond Bingo
• Bolster students' learning by bringing in objects that represent the shapes on their calling cards, such as building blocks, bathroom tissue rolls, funnels, and so on. When a calling card is chosen, ask players to find the corresponding shape on both their bingo cards and in your collection.

• Invite students to compare and contrast the calling card shapes. You may ask, "How is the shape of a juice can like the shape of a paper-towel roll?" or "How is the shape of the tent different from the shape of the ice cream cone?"

• Have students create sculptures using their calling card shapes. Some might represent real-life structures—for example, a house and a roof—while others might be make-believe.

Game Set 7 (Simple Fractions)
Students match the shaded portions of shapes to the corresponding fractions on the calling cards. To vary play, challenge students to match the unshaded portions of the shapes to the fractions on the calling cards.

Beyond Bingo
• Have students trace and cut out from cardboard enlarged versions of the simple geometric shapes on their bingo boards. Using a felt-tip pen, students can divide the shapes into portions that correspond to the fractions on the calling cards (halves, thirds, quarters). Then ask students to cut the shapes apart. Allow them ample time to manipulate the shapes—taking them apart, putting them back together, and counting the pieces—to give them a better sense of these part/whole relationships.

• For additional reinforcement, give a copy of the blank calling card page to each student. Invite students to draw and divide simple shapes to create their own illustrated fraction calling cards.

• Create your own bingo boards and calling cards to show additional fractions such as sixths or eighths. Use very simple shapes like circles, squares, and rectangles. Challenge your students to play these more advanced bingo games.

Game Set 8 (Time Showing the Hour and Half Hour)
Game Set 9 (Time Showing Quarter Of and Quarter After the Hour)
These game sets include bingo boards with analog clocks that students must match to digital times on the calling cards.

Beyond Bingo

• Provide students with analog clock faces made from cardboard. Attach a minute hand and an hour hand to the center of each clock face using a brass fastener. Draw minute marks along the edge of each clock face. When calling cards are drawn, players should show the corresponding time on their clock faces before locating them on their bingo boards.

• Ask students to create verbal clues to replace the calling cards. For example, if the calling card for 11:30 were drawn, the student who chose the card might ask, "What is one hour before 12:30?" or "What is two hours after 9:30?" Students might even offer clues, such as "At this time we're usually eating lunch."

Game Set 10 (Counting Coins) and Game Set 11 (Counting Dollar Bills and Coins)

Players match the value of coin and dollar arrays on their bingo boards to the monetary values written on the calling cards.

Beyond Bingo

• Invite students to calculate calling card totals, using real or play money, before they make matches on their bingo boards.

• Challenge children to come up with additional coin or dollar combinations that yield the amount on the calling cards. For example, if the calling card for $1.00 is chosen and a player has 3 quarters, 1 dime, and 3 nickels, after he puts a token on that space, he might offer, "Another way to make a dollar is with 4 quarters."

• Invite students to go on a mini shopping spree. Price some items in your classroom and challenge children to tell you whether they have enough money on their board (or in one column or row) to afford each item.

Game Set 12 (Greater Than/Less Than)

In this game, each calling card has two numbers separated by a space—for example, 8 __ 10. Players must decide if 8 is less than or greater than 10 and must place a token over the corresponding symbol on their bingo boards. While playing this game, it is particularly important to remind players that once they have placed a token on a space, they cannot move it.

Beyond Bingo

• Ask players to use simple counters, such as buttons, beans, or pasta, to show the comparisons on the calling cards.

• Create calling cards that compare two-digit numbers such as 23 and 27, and challenge students to play.

However you and your students decide to play, we hope you will enjoy this winning way to reinforce essential math skills and have fun!

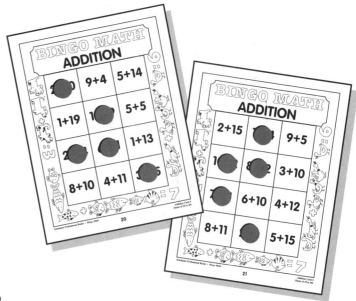

Ways to Win at Bingo

BINGO MATH
ADDITION

1+4	3+6	5+2
3+0	2+2	0+0
8+2	5+4	6+2
4+2	2+0	0+1

Addition Card 1
(Sums of 0 to 10)

BINGO MATH
ADDITION

7+2	2+1	6+4
0+0	3+3	2+0
2+6	4+1	0+1
5+5	2+2	0+7

Addition Card 2
(Sums of 0 to 10)

BINGO MATH
ADDITION

3+0	1+1	7+0
0+6	0+4	2+7
1+0	2+3	7+3
2+4	0+0	4+4

BINGO MATH
ADDITION

3+1	8+0	5+1
1+0	8+1	4+3
1+2	4+6	0+0
7+1	0+2	3+2

Addition Card 4
(Sums of 0 to 10)

BINGO MATH
ADDITION

0+1	0+0	2+1
1+5	5+0	3+5
2+8	1+3	1+9
6+1	0+2	4+5

Scholastic Professional Books • *Bingo Math*

Addition Card 5
(Sums of 0 to 10)

BINGO MATH
ADDITION

3+0	1+0	1+1
0+5	6+0	5+3
0+0	9+1	0+10
4+0	1+8	2+5

0	1
2	3
4	5
6	7
8	9
10	

BINGO MATH
ADDITION

1+16 17	**7+10** 17	**7+13** 20
2+11 13	**5+11** 16	**3+12** 15
2+10 12	**5+9** 14	**2+17** 19
4+14 18	**1+10** 11	**9+9** 18

BINGO MATH
ADDITION

5+12 *17*	3+9 *12*	6+4 *10*
4+15 *19*	10+10 *20*	6+13 *19*
7+4 *11*	2+12 *14*	2+18 *20*
4+9 *13*	1+17 *18*	3+13 *16*

BINGO MATH
ADDITION

2+13	8+3	6+12
4+10	4+16	7+9
3+8	1+12	1+18
5+13	8+2	11+1

BINGO MATH
ADDITION

2+10	9+4	5+14
1+19	10+9	5+5
2+14	6+11	1+13
8+10	4+11	3+15

Scholastic Professional Books • *Bingo Math*

Addition Card 4
(Sums of 10 to 20)

BINGO MATH
ADDITION

2+15	1+14	9+5
10+2	8+12	3+10
7+11	6+10	4+12
8+11	2+9	5+15

BINGO MATH
ADDITION

3+7	3+16	5+10
2+16	6+5	1+15
12+1	4+13	6+14
3+17	9+2	1+11

10	**11**
12	**13**
14	**15**
16	**17**
18	**19**
20	

BINGO MATH
SUBTRACTION

4-1 *3*	6-4 *2*	7-2 *5*
10-10 *0*	10-2 *8*	3-2 *1*
9-0 *9*	6-2 *4*	8-1 *7*
9-8 *1*	5-2 *3*	10-0 *10*

BINGO MATH
SUBTRACTION

3-3	9-1	6-1
9-0	10-3	9-9
3-0	7-5	8-7
6-0	5-1	10-0

BINGO MATH
SUBTRACTION

7-7	9-0	9-5
10-0	10-4	7-4
8-0	1-1	9-2
6-5	10-5	4-2

BINGO MATH
SUBTRACTION

8-4	9-3	0-0
3-1	10-1	8-0
9-4	10-0	9-7
6-3	8-1	5-4

BINGO MATH
SUBTRACTION

2-2	10-3	8-5
9-0	10-2	4-0
7-1	5-0	5-3
7-6	8-8	10-0

BINGO MATH
SUBTRACTION

8-2	10-0	7-0
10-7	4-3	9-1
8-6	7-3	10-1
5-5	8-3	2-0

0	1
2	3
4	5
6	7
8	9
10	

BINGO MATH
SUBTRACTION

18-0	**11-1**	**16-5**
19-2	**17-2**	**14-4**
20-0	**18-4**	**19-0**
15-2	**13-1**	**20-4**

BINGO MATH
SUBTRACTION

17-6	18-2	16-4
20-0	19-4	13-3
19-6	14-2	20-1
16-2	17-0	19-1

BINGO MATH
SUBTRACTION

18-1	**20-0**	**15-4**
13-2	**17-3**	**19-7**
12-2	**17-1**	**14-1**
20-2	**18-3**	**19-0**

BINGO MATH
SUBTRACTION

20-3	16-1	15-5
18-0	14-3	17-4
18-6	20-1	19-5
20-0	12-1	16-0

BINGO MATH
SUBTRACTION

19-3	15-1	19-0
17-5	20-0	16-6
20-5	12-0	18-7
19-1	18-5	20-3

BINGO MATH
SUBTRACTION

15-3	20-1	11-0
18-8	14-0	16-3
18-2	15-0	20-2
18-1	20-0	19-8

10

11

12

13

14

15

16

17

18

19

20

BINGO MATH
2-D SHAPES

BINGO MATH
2-D SHAPES

BINGO MATH
2-D SHAPES

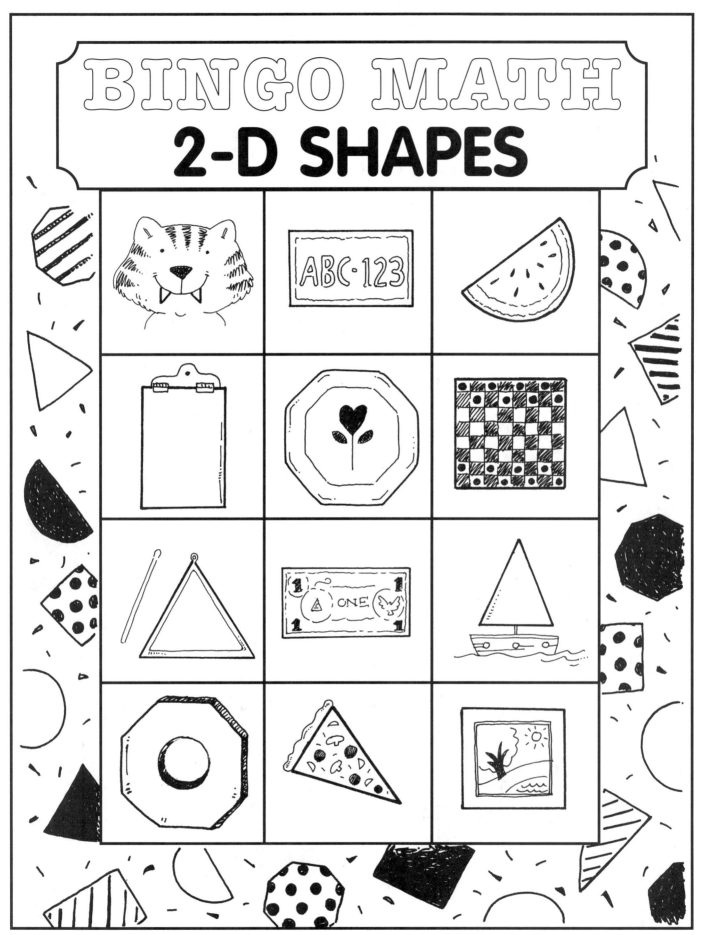

BINGO MATH
2-D SHAPES

BINGO MATH
2-D SHAPES

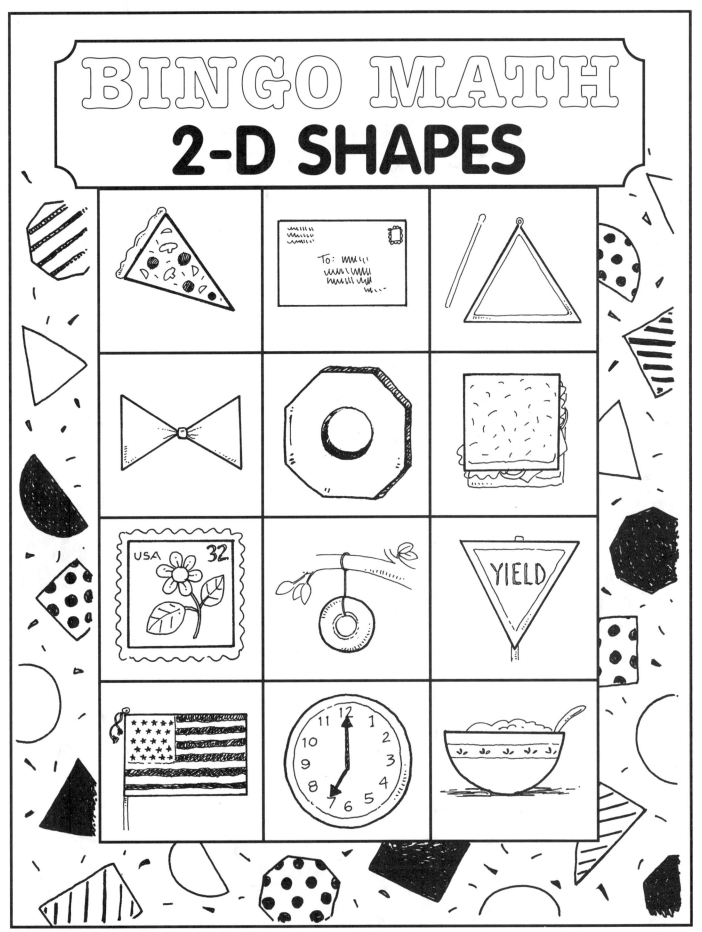

BINGO MATH
2-D SHAPES

2-D Shapes Calling Cards

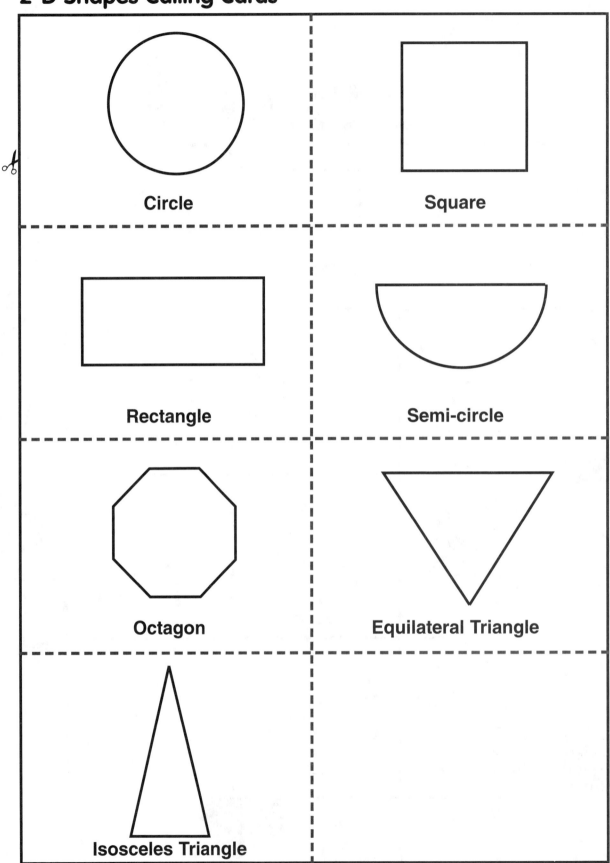

Circle

Square

Rectangle

Semi-circle

Octagon

Equilateral Triangle

Isosceles Triangle

BINGO MATH
3-D SHAPES

BINGO MATH
3-D SHAPES

BINGO MATH
3-D SHAPES

BINGO MATH
3-D SHAPES

BINGO MATH
3-D SHAPES

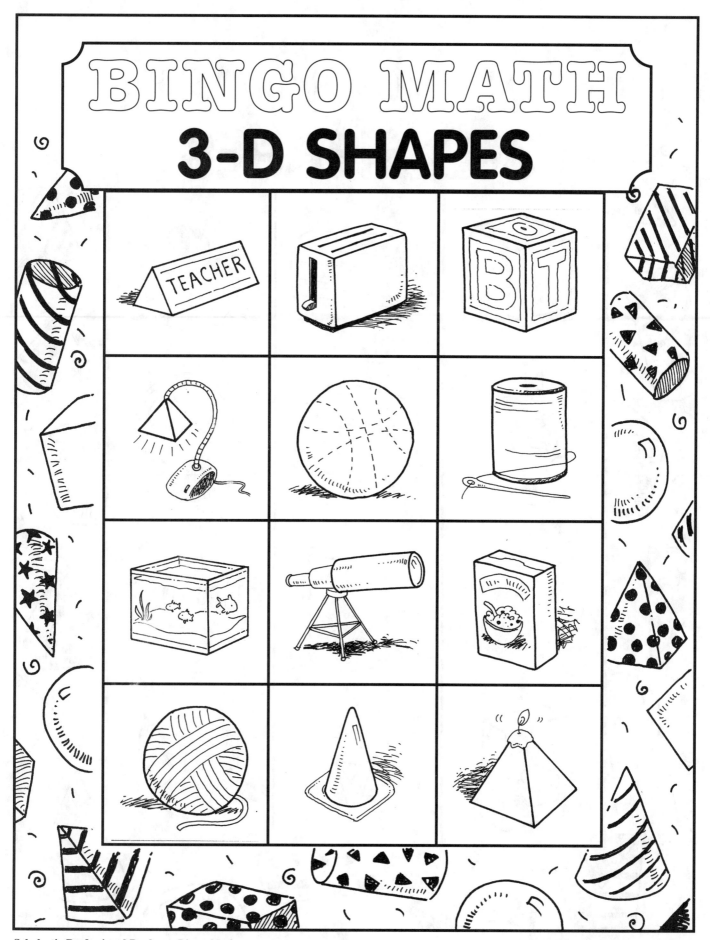

BINGO MATH
3-D SHAPES

3-D Shapes Call-Out Cards

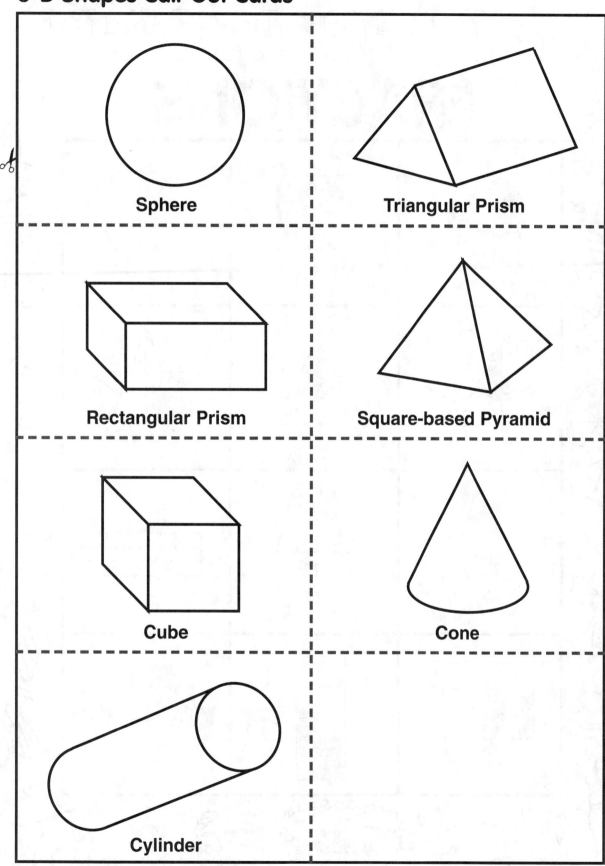

Sphere

Triangular Prism

Rectangular Prism

Square-based Pyramid

Cube

Cone

Cylinder

BINGO MATH
FRACTIONS

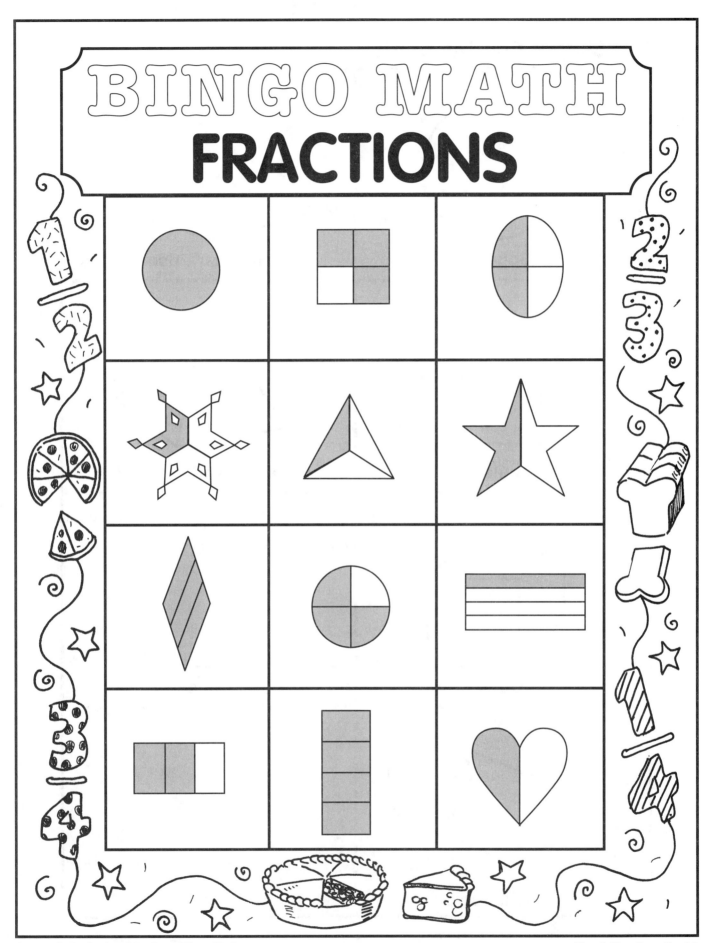

Scholastic Professional Books • *Bingo Math*

Simple Fractions Card 1

BINGO MATH
FRACTIONS

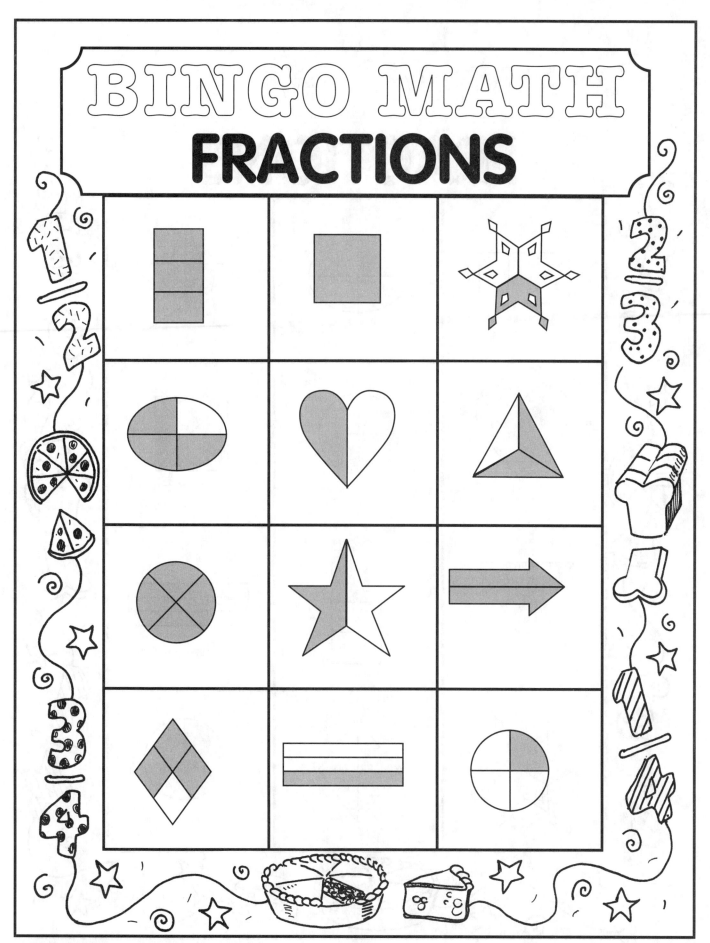

BINGO MATH
FRACTIONS

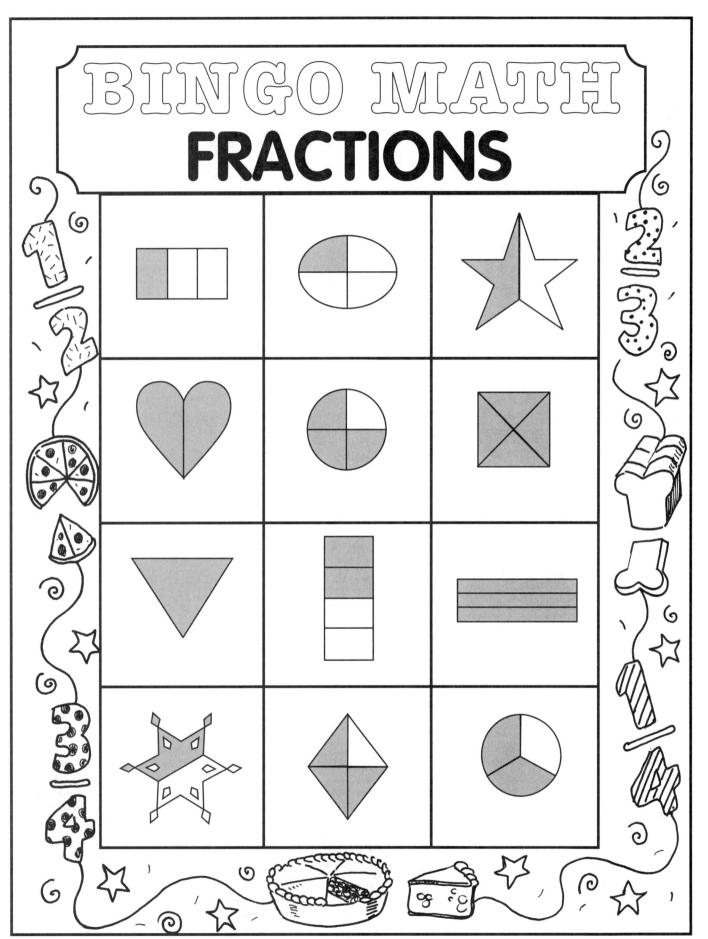

BINGO MATH
FRACTIONS

BINGO MATH
FRACTIONS

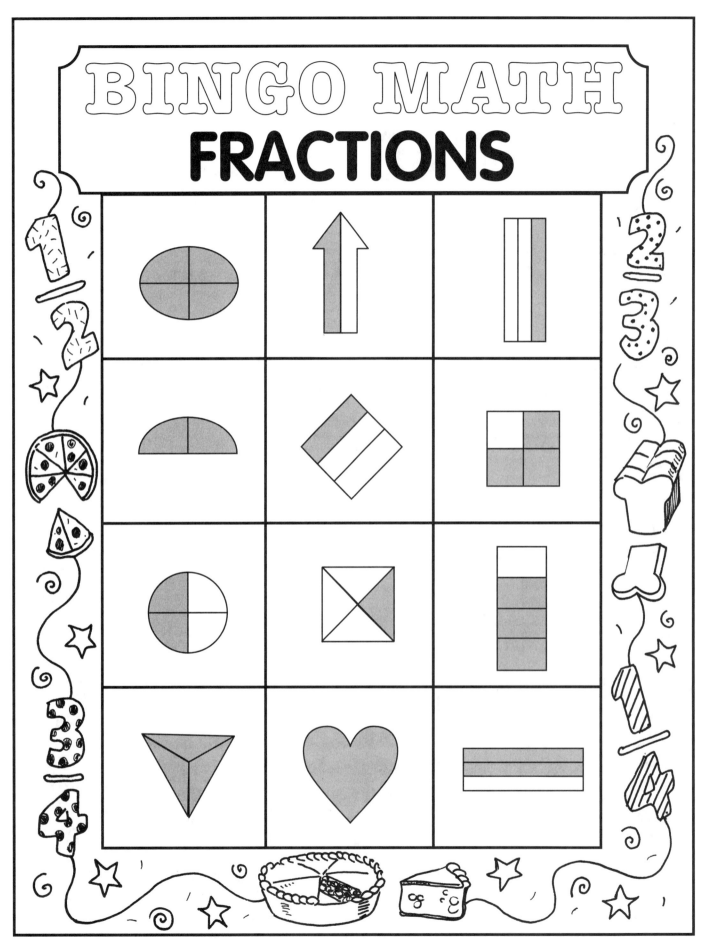

BINGO MATH
FRACTIONS

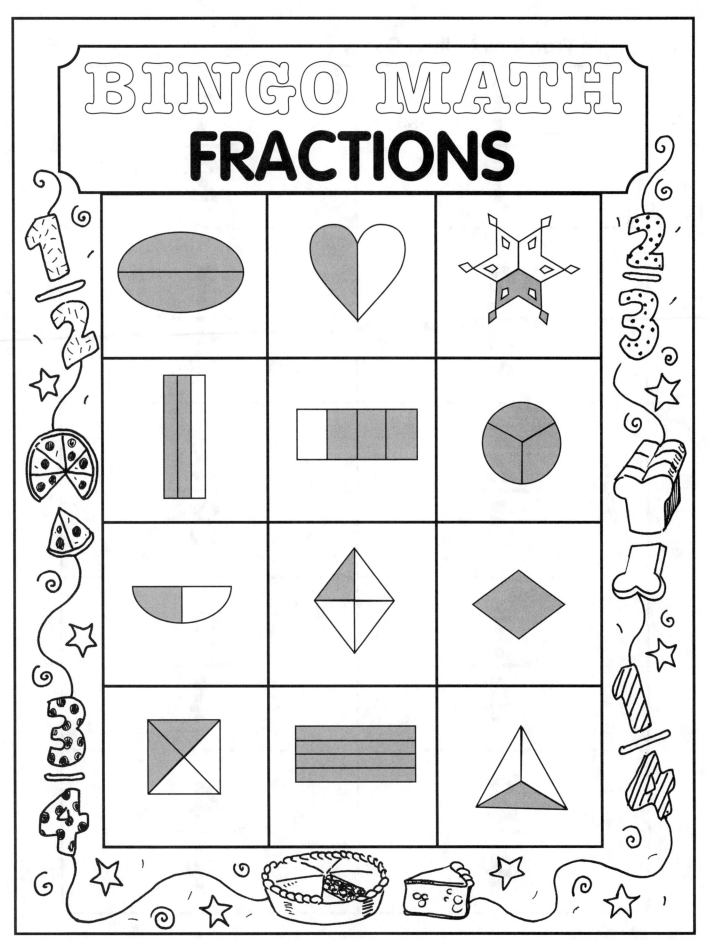

Simple Fractions Calling Cards

$\dfrac{1}{1}$	$\dfrac{1}{2}$
$\dfrac{2}{2}$	$\dfrac{1}{3}$
$\dfrac{2}{3}$	$\dfrac{3}{3}$
$\dfrac{1}{4}$	$\dfrac{2}{4}$
$\dfrac{3}{4}$	$\dfrac{4}{4}$

BINGO MATH
TIME

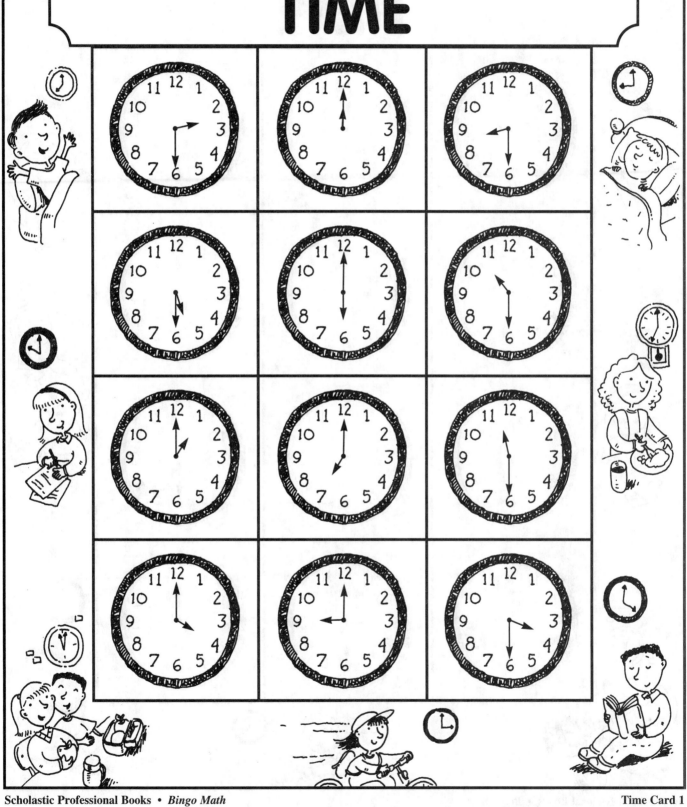

BINGO MATH
TIME

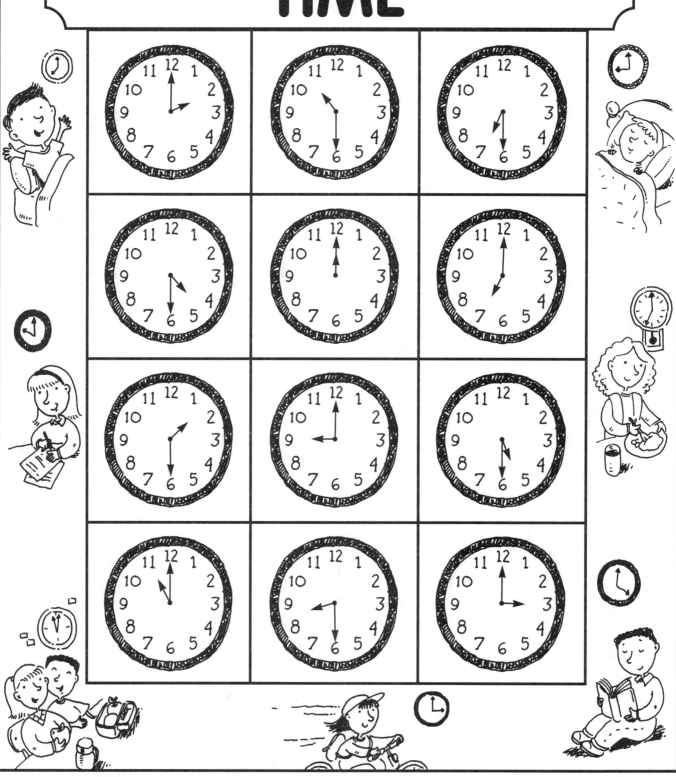

BINGO MATH
TIME

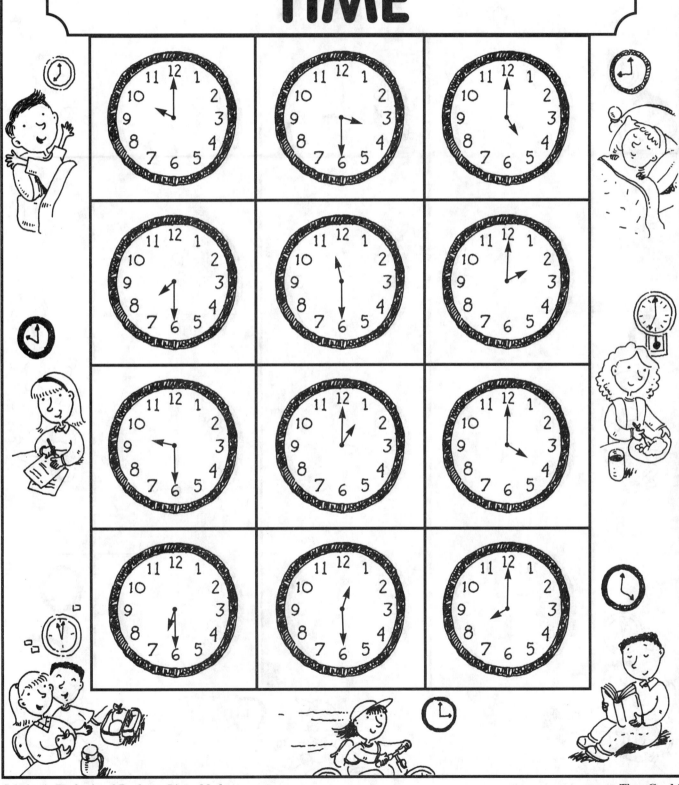

BINGO MATH
TIME

BINGO MATH
TIME

BINGO MATH
TIME

Time Calling Cards   (Showing the Hour & Half Hour)

1:00	9:00	5:30
2:00	10:00	6:30
3:00	11:00	7:30
4:00	12:00	8:30
5:00	1:30	9:30
6:00	2:30	10:30
7:00	3:30	11:30
8:00	4:30	12:30

BINGO MATH
TIME

BINGO MATH
TIME

BINGO MATH
TIME

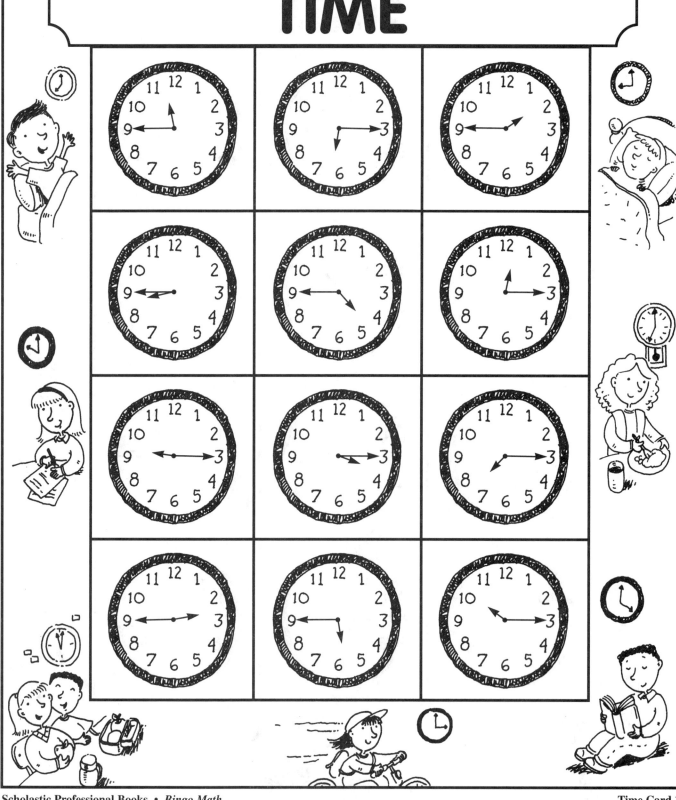

BINGO MATH
TIME

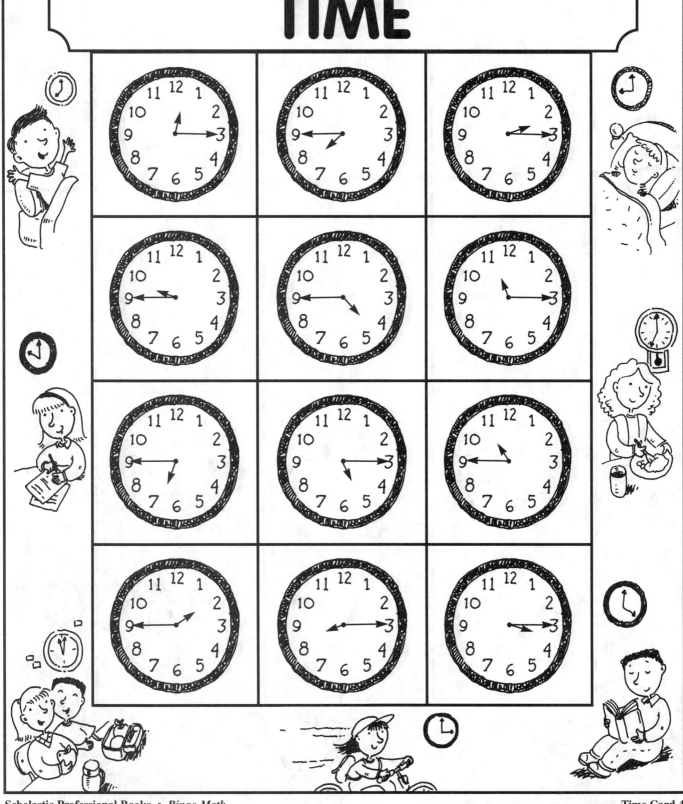

BINGO MATH
TIME

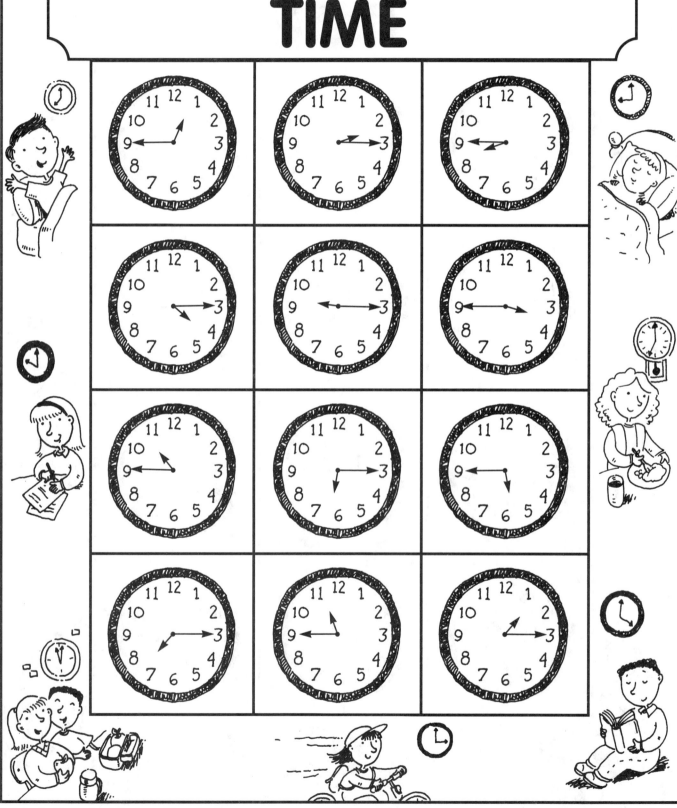

BINGO MATH
TIME

1:15	**9:15**	**5:45**
2:15	**10:15**	**6:45**
3:15	**11:15**	**7:45**
4:15	**12:15**	**8:45**
5:15	**1:45**	**9:45**
6:15	**2:45**	**10:45**
7:15	**3:45**	**11:45**
8:15	**4:45**	**12:45**

BINGO MATH
MONEY

BINGO MATH
MONEY

BINGO MATH
MONEY

BINGO MATH
MONEY

BINGO MATH
MONEY

BINGO MATH
MONEY

3¢	49¢
7¢	50¢
10¢	62¢
18¢	75¢
20¢	86¢
25¢	$1.00

BINGO MATH
MONEY

BINGO MATH
MONEY

BINGO MATH
MONEY

Money Card 3
(Counting Dollar Bills and Coins)

BINGO MATH
MONEY

BINGO MATH
MONEY

BINGO MATH
MONEY

$1.00	**$1.94**
$1.03	**$2.00**
$1.10	**$2.15**
$1.25	**$2.50**
$1.34	**$2.77**
$1.48	**$3.00**

BINGO MATH
GREATER THAN / LESS THAN

Scholastic Professional Books • *Bingo Math*

Greater Than and Less Than Card 1

87

BINGO MATH
GREATER THAN / LESS THAN

BINGO MATH
GREATER THAN / LESS THAN

BINGO MATH
GREATER THAN / LESS THAN

BINGO MATH
GREATER THAN / LESS THAN

BINGO MATH
GREATER THAN / LESS THAN

<	>	<
>	>	<
<	>	<
>	>	<

Greater Than / Less Than Call-Out Cards

8 __ 10	7 __ 2
4 __ 3	6 __ 0
1 __ 6	5 __ 6
6 __ 8	2 __ 1
3 __ 5	8 __ 5
9 __ 7	7 __ 9

Tokens

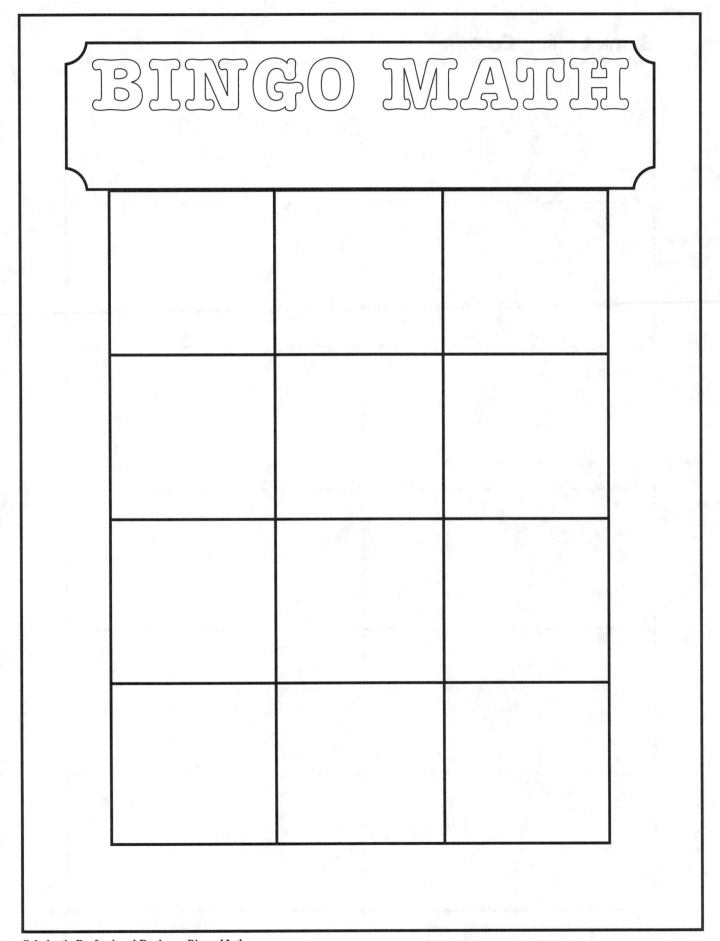

BINGO MATH

Blank Calling Cards